IMMORTALITY OF THE SOUL OR RESURRECTION OF THE DEAD?

THE WITNESS OF THE NEW TESTAMENT

IMMORTALITY OF THE SOUL OR RESURRECTION OF THE DEAD?

The Witness of the New Testament

OSCAR CULLMANN, D.TH., D.D.
Professor of the Theological Faculty of the University of Basel and of the Sorbonne in Paris

London
THE EPWORTH PRESS

FIRST PUBLISHED IN 1958

Book Steward
FRANK H. CUMBERS

THE INGERSOLL LECTURE ON
THE IMMORTALITY OF MAN
FOR THE ACADEMIC YEAR 1954-55
HARVARD UNIVERSITY

DELIVERED IN ANDOVER CHAPEL 26th APRIL 1955

SET IN MONOTYPE CASLON AND PRINTED IN
GREAT BRITAIN BY THE CAMELOT PRESS LTD
LONDON AND SOUTHAMPTON

PREFACE

THE PRESENT work is the translation of a study already published in Switzerland,[1] of which a summary has appeared in various French periodicals.

No other publication of mine has provoked such enthusiasm or such violent hostility. The editors of the periodicals concerned have been good enough to send me some of the letters of protest which they have received from their readers. One of the letter-writers was prompted by my article to reflect bitterly that 'the French people, dying for lack of the Bread of Life, have been offered instead of bread, stones, if not serpents'. Another writer takes me for a kind of monster who delights in causing spiritual distress. 'Has M. Cullmann', he writes, 'a stone instead of a heart?' For a third, my study has been 'the cause of astonishment, sorrow, and deep distress'. Friends who have followed my previous work with interest and approval have indicated to me the pain which this study has caused them. In others I have detected a malaise which they have tried to conceal by an eloquent silence.

My critics belong to the most varied camps. The

[1] *Mélanges* offerts à KARL BARTH à l'occasion de ses 70 ans (publ. by Reinhardt, Bâle, 1956) (*Theologische Zeitschrift*, N. 2, pp. 126ff). See also *Verbum Caro* (1956), pp. 58ff.

contrast, which out of concern for the truth I have found it necessary to draw between the courageous and joyful primitive Christian hope of the resurrection of the dead and the serene philosophic expectation of the survival of the immortal soul, has displeased not only many sincere Christians in all Communions and of all theological outlooks, but also those whose convictions, while not outwardly alienated from Christianity, are more strongly moulded by philosophical considerations. So far, no critic of either kind has attempted to refute me by exegesis, that being the basis of our study.

This remarkable agreement seems to me to show how widespread is the mistake of attributing to primitive Christianity the Greek belief in the immortality of the soul. Further, people with such different attitudes as those I have mentioned are united in a common inability to *listen* with complete objectivity to what the texts teach us about the faith and hope of primitive Christianity, without mixing their own opinions and the views that are so dear to them with their interpretation of the texts. This inability to listen is equally surprising on the part of intelligent people committed to the principles of sound, scientific exegesis and on the part of believers who profess to rely on the revelation in Holy Scripture.

The attacks provoked by my work would impress me more if they were based on exegetical arguments. Instead, I am attacked with very general considerations of a philosophical, psychological, and above all sentimental kind. It has been said against me, 'I can accept the immortality of the soul, but not the resurrection of the body', or 'I cannot believe that our loved ones merely sleep for an indeterminate period, and that I myself, when I die, shall merely sleep while awaiting the resurrection'.

Is it really necessary today to remind intelligent people, whether Christians or not, that there is a difference between recognizing that such a view was held by Socrates and accepting it, between recognizing a hope as primitive Christian and sharing it oneself?

We must first listen to what Plato and St Paul said. We can go farther. We can respect and indeed admire both views. How can we fail to do so when we see them in relation to the life and death of their authors? But that is no reason for denying a radical difference between the Christian expectation of the resurrection of the dead and the Greek belief in the immortality of the soul. However sincere our admiration for both views, it cannot allow us to pretend, against our profound conviction and against the exegetical evidence, that they are compatible. That it is possible to discover certain points of contact, I have shown in this study; but that does not prevent their fundamental inspiration being totally different.

The fact that later Christianity effected a link between the two beliefs and that today the ordinary Christian simply confuses them has not persuaded me to be silent about what I, in common with most exegetes, regard as true; and all the more so, since the link established between the expectation of the 'resurrection of the dead' and the belief in 'the immortality of the soul' is not in fact a link at all but renunciation of one in favour of the other. 1 Corinthians 15 has been sacrificed for the *Phaedo*. No good purpose is served by concealing this fact, as is often done today when things that are really imcompatible are combined by the following type of over-simplified reasoning: that whatever in early Christian teaching appears to us irreconcilable with the immortality of the soul, viz. the resurrection of the body, is not an *essential* affirmation for the first Christians but simply an accommodation to the mythological expressions of the thought of their time, and that the heart of the matter is the immortality of the soul. On the contrary we must recognize loyally that precisely those things which distinguish the Christian teaching from the Greek belief are at the heart of primitive Christianity. Even if the interpreter cannot himself accept it as fundamental, he has no right to conclude that it was not fundamental for the authors whom he studies.

. . . . .

In view of the negative reactions and 'distress' provoked by the publication of my thesis in various periodicals, should I not have broken off the debate for the sake of Christian charity, instead of publishing this booklet? My decision has been determined by the conviction that 'stumbling-blocks' are sometimes salutary, both from the scholarly and the Christian point of view. I simply ask my readers to be good enough to take the trouble of reading on till the end.

The question is here raised in its exegetical aspect. If we turn to the Christian aspect, I would venture to remind my critics that when they put in the forefront, as they do, the particular manner in which they *wish* themselves and their loved ones to survive, they are involuntarily giving grounds to the opponents of Christianity who constantly repeat that the faith of Christians is nothing more than the projection of their desires.

In reality, does it not belong to the greatness of our Christian faith, as I have done my best to expound it, that we do not begin from our personal desires but place our resurrection within the framework of a cosmic redemption and of a new creation of the universe?

I do not under-estimate in any way the difficulty one may experience in sharing this faith, and I freely admit the difficulty of talking about this subject in a dispassionate manner. An open grave at once reminds us that we are not simply concerned with a matter of academic discussion. But is there not therefore all the more reason for seeking truth and clarity at this point? The best way to do it is not by beginning with what is ambiguous, but by explaining simply and as faithfully as possible, with all the means at our disposal, the hope of the New Testament authors, and thus showing the very essence of this hope and—however hard it may seem to us—what it is that separates it from other beliefs we hold so dear. If in the first place we examine objectively the primitive Christian expectation in those aspects which seem shocking to our commonly accepted views, are we not following the only possible way by which it may perhaps none the less be given us, not only to understand that expectation better, but also to ascertain that it is not so impossible to accept it as we imagine.

I have the impression that some of my readers have not troubled to read my exposition right through. The comparison of the death of Socrates with that of Jesus seems to have scandalized and irritated them so much that they have read no farther, and have not looked at what I have said about the New Testament faith in the victory of Christ over death.

For many of those who have attacked me the cause of 'sorrow and distress' has been not only the distinction we draw between resurrection of the dead and immortality of the soul, but above all the place which I with the whole of primitive Christianity believe should be given to the intermediate state of those who are dead and die in Christ before the final days, the state which the first-century authors described by the word 'sleep'. The idea of a temporary state of waiting is all the more repugnant to those who would like fuller information about this 'sleep' of the dead who, though stripped of their fleshly bodies, are still deprived of their resurrection bodies although in possession of the Holy Spirit. They are not able to observe the discretion of the New Testament authors, including St Paul, in this matter; or to be satisfied with the joyful assurance of the Apostle when he says that henceforth death can no longer separate from Christ him who has the Holy Spirit. 'Whether we live or die, we belong to Christ.'

There are some who find this idea of 'sleep' entirely unacceptable. I am tempted to lay aside for a moment the exegetical methods of this study and ask them whether they have never experienced a dream which has made them happier than any other experience, even though they have only been sleeping. Might that not be an illustration, though indeed an imperfect one, of the state of anticipation in which, according to St Paul, the dead in Christ find themselves during their 'sleeping' as they wait for the resurrection of the body?

However that may be, I do not intend to avoid the 'stumbling-block' by minimizing what I have said about the provisional and still imperfect character of this state. The fact is that, according to the first Christians the full, genuine life of the resurrection is inconceivable apart from the new body, the 'spiritual body', with which the dead will be clothed when heaven and earth are re-created.

In this study I have referred more than once to the Isenheim altar-piece by the medieval painter Grünewald. It was the resurrection body that he depicted, not the immortal soul. Similarly, another artist, John Sebastian Bach, has made it possible for us to hear, in the Credo of the Mass in B Minor, the musical interpretation of the words of this ancient creed which faithfully reproduces the New Testament faith in Christ's resurrection and our own. The jubilant music of this great composer is intended to express not the immortality of the soul but the event of the resurrection of the body: *Et resurrexit tertia die . . . Expecto resurrectionem mortuorum et vitam venturi saeculi.* And Handel, in the last part of the *Messiah*, gives us some inkling of what St Paul understood by the sleep of those who rest in Christ; and also, in the song of triumph, Paul's expectation of the final resurrection when the 'last trumpet shall sound and we shall be changed'.

Whether we share this hope or not, let us at least admit that in this case the artists have proved the best expositors of the Bible.

CHAMONIX
15th September 1956

CONTENTS

INTRODUCTION

If we were to ask an ordinary Christian today (whether well-read Protestant or Catholic, or not) what he conceived to be the New Testament teaching concerning the fate of man after death, with few exceptions we should get the answer: 'The immortality of the soul.' Yet this widely-accepted idea is one of the greatest misunderstandings of Christianity. There is no point in attempting to hide this fact, or to veil it by reinterpreting the Christian faith. This is something that should be discussed quite candidly. The concept of death and resurrection is anchored in the Christ-event (as will be shown in the following pages), and hence is incompatible with the Greek belief in immortality; because it is based in *Heilsgeschichte* it is offensive to modern thought. Is it not such an integral element of the early Christian proclamation that it can neither be surrendered nor reinterpreted without robbing the New Testament of its substance?[1]

But is it really true that the early Christian resurrection faith is irreconcilable with the Greek concept of

[1] See on the following also O. Cullmann, 'La foi à la résurrection et l'espérance de la résurrection dans le Nouveau Testament', *Etudes théol. et rel* (1943), pp. 3ff; *Christ and Time* (1945), pp. 231ff; Ph. H. Menoud, *Le sort des trépassés* (1945); R. Mehl, *Der letzte Feind* (1954).

the immortality of the soul? Does not the New Testament, and above all the Gospel of John, teach that we already have eternal life? Is it really true that death in the New Testament is always conceived as 'the last enemy' in a way that is diametrically opposed to Greek thought, which sees in death a friend? Does not Paul write: 'O death, where is thy sting?' We shall see at the end that there *is* at least an analogy, but first we must stress the fundamental differences between the two points of view.

The widespread misunderstanding that the New Testament teaches the immortality of the soul was actually encouraged by the rock-like *post-Easter* conviction of the first disciples that the bodily Resurrection of Christ had robbed death of all its horror,[2] and that from the moment of Easter onward, the Holy Spirit had awakened the souls of believers into the life of the Resurrection.

The very fact that the words '*post-Easter*' need to be underlined illustrates the whole abyss which nevertheless separates the early Christian view from that of the Greeks. The whole of early Christian thought is based in *Heilsgeschichte*, and everything that is said about death and eternal life stands or falls with a belief in a real occurrence, in real events which took place in

[2] But hardly in such a way that the original Christian community could speak of 'natural' dying. This manner of speaking of Karl Barth's in *Die kirchliche Dogmatik*, III, 2 (1948), pp. 776ff, though found in a section where otherwise the negative valuation of death as the 'last enemy' is strongly emphasized, still seems to me not to be grounded in the New Testament. See 1 Corinthians 11[30] (on that verse see below, pp. 34, 37).

time. This is the radical distinction from Greek thought. The purpose of my book *Christ and Time* was precisely to show that this belongs to the substance, to the essence of early Christian faith, that it is something not to be surrendered, not to be altered in meaning; yet it has often been mistakenly thought that I intended to write an essay on the New Testament attitude toward the problem of Time and Eternity.

If one recognizes that death and eternal life in the New Testament are always bound up with the Christ-event, then it becomes clear that for the first Christians the soul is not intrinsically immortal, but rather became so only through the resurrection of Jesus Christ, and through faith in Him. It also becomes clear that death is not intrinsically the Friend, but rather that its 'sting', its power, is taken away *only* through the victory of Jesus over it in His death. And lastly, it becomes clear that the resurrection already accomplished is not the state of fulfilment, for that remains in the future until the body is also resurrected, which will not occur until 'the last day'.

It is a mistake to read into the Fourth Gospel an early trend toward the Greek teaching of immortality, because there also eternal life is bound up with the Christ-event.[3] Within the bounds of the Christ-event, of course, the various New Testament books place the accent in different places, but common to all is the view

[3] In so far as John's Gospel is rooted in *Heilsgeschichte*, it is not true, as Rudolf Bultmann wrongly maintains, that a process of demythologizing is already to be discerned in it.

of *Heilsgeschichte*.[4] Obviously one must reckon with Greek influence upon the origin of Christianity from the very beginning,[5] but so long as the Greek ideas are subordinated to the total view of *Heilsgeschichte*, there can be no talk of 'Hellenization' in the proper sense.[6] Genuine Hellenization occurs for the first time at a later date.

[4] As Bo Reicke correctly maintains, 'Einheitlichkeit oder verschiedene Lehrbegriffe in der neutestamentlichen Theologie', *Theol. Zeitschr.*, 9 (1953), pp. 401ff.

[5] All the more as the Qumrân texts show that the Judaism to which embryonic Christianity was so closely connected was already itself influenced by Hellenism. See O. Cullmann, 'The Significance of the Qumrân Texts for Research into the Beginnings of Christianity', *Journ. of Bibl. Lit.*, 74 (1955), pp. 213ff. So too Rudolf Bultmann, *Theology of the New Testament* (1955), Vol. II, p. 13 note.

[6] Rather, it would be more accurate to speak of a Christian 'historicization' (in the sense of *Heilsgeschichte*) of the Greek ideas. Only in this sense, not in that employed by Bultmann, are the New Testament 'myths' already 'demythologized' by the New Testament itself.

I

THE LAST ENEMY: DEATH

SOCRATES AND JESUS

NOTHING SHOWS more clearly than the contrast between the death of Socrates and that of Jesus (a contrast which was often cited, though for other purposes, by early opponents of Christianity) that the biblical view of death from the first is focused in salvation-history and so departs completely from the Greek conception.[1]

In Plato's impressive description of the death of Socrates, in the *Phaedo*, occurs perhaps the highest and most sublime doctrine ever presented on the immortality of the soul. What gives his argument its unexcelled value is his scientific reserve, his disclaimer of any proof having mathematical validity. We know the arguments he offers for the immortality of the soul. Our body is only an outer garment which, as long as we live, prevents our soul from moving freely and from living in conformity to its proper eternal essence. It imposes upon the soul a law which is not appropriate to it. The soul, confined within the body, belongs to

[1] Material on this contrast in E. Benz, *Der gekreuzigte Gerechte bei Plato im N.T. und in der alten Kirche* (1950).

the eternal world. As long as we live, our soul finds itself in a prison, that is, in a body essentially alien to it. Death, in fact, is the great liberator. It looses the chains, since it leads the soul out of the prison of the body and back to its eternal home. Since body and soul are radically different from one another and belong to different worlds, the destruction of the body cannot mean the destruction of the soul, any more than a musical composition can be destroyed when the instrument is destroyed. Although the proofs of the immortality of the soul do not have for Socrates himself the same value as the proofs of a mathematical theorem, they nevertheless attain within their own sphere the highest possible degree of validity, and make immortality so probable that it amounts to a 'fair chance' for man. And when the great Socrates traced the arguments for immortality in his address to his disciples on the day of his death, he did not merely *teach* this doctrine: at that moment he lived his doctrine. He showed how we serve the freedom of the soul, even in this present life, when we occupy ourselves with the eternal truths of philosophy. For through philosophy we penetrate into that eternal world of ideas to which the soul belongs, and we free the soul from the prison of the body. Death does no more than complete this liberation. Plato shows us how Socrates goes to his death in complete peace and composure. The death of Socrates is a beautiful death. Nothing is seen here of death's terror. Socrates cannot fear death, since indeed it sets us free from the body. Whoever fears death proves that he loves the world of the body, that he is thoroughly entangled in the world of sense. Death is the soul's great friend. So he teaches; and so, in wonderful harmony with his teaching, he dies—this man who embodied the Greek world in its noblest form.

And now let us hear how Jesus dies. In Gethsemane He knows that death stands before Him, just as Socrates expected death on his last day. The Synoptic Evangelists furnish us, by and large, with a unanimous report. Jesus begins 'to tremble and be distressed', writes Mark (14^{33}). 'My soul is troubled, even to death', He says to His disciples.[2] Jesus is so thoroughly human that He shares the natural fear of death.[3] Jesus

[2] Despite the parallel Jonah 4^{9} which is cited by E. Klostermann, *Das Markus-Evangelium*, 3rd Edition (1936), ad loc., and E. Lohmeyer, *Das Evangelium des Markus* (1937), ad loc., I agree with J. Weiss, *Das Markus-Evangelium*, 3rd Edition (1917), ad loc., that the explanation: 'I am so sad that I prefer to die' in this situation where Jesus *knows* that He is going to die (the scene is the Last Supper!) is completely unsatisfactory; moreover, Weiss's interpretation: 'My affliction is so great that I am sinking under the weight of it' is supported by Mark 15^{34}. Also Luke 12^{50}, 'How distressed I am until the baptism (=death) takes place', allows of no other explanation.

[3] Old and recent commentators (J. Wellhausen, *Das Evangelium Marci*, 2nd Edition (1909), ad. loc., J. Schniewind in *N.T. Deutsch* (1934), ad. loc., E. Lohmeyer, *Das Evangelium des Markus* (1937), ad loc., seek in vain to avoid this conclusion, which is supported by the strong Greek expressions for 'tremble and shrink', by giving explanations which do not fit the situation, in which Jesus already knows that He must suffer for the sins of His people (Last Supper). In Luke 12^{50} it is completely impossible to explain away the 'distress' in the face of death, and also in view of the fact that Jesus is abandoned by God on the Cross (Mark 15^{34}), it is not possible to explain the Gethsemane scene except through this distress at the prospect of being abandoned by God, an abandonment which will be the work of Death, God's great enemy.

is afraid, though not as a coward would be of the men who will kill Him, still less of the pain and grief which precede death. He is afraid in the face of death itself. Death for Him is not something divine : it is something dreadful. Jesus does not want to be alone in this moment. He knows, of course, that the Father stands by to help Him. He looks to Him in this decisive moment as He has done throughout his life. He turns to Him with all His human fear of this great enemy, death. He is afraid of death. It is useless to try to explain away Jesus' fear as reported by the Evangelists. The opponents of Christianity who already in the first centuries made the contrast between the death of Socrates and the death of Jesus saw more clearly here than the exponents of Christianity. He was really afraid. Here is nothing of the composure of Socrates, who met death peacefully as a friend. To be sure, Jesus already knows the task which has been given Him : to suffer death; and He has already spoken the words: 'I have a baptism with which I must be baptized, and *how distressed* (or *afraid*) *I am* until it is accomplished' (Luke 19[50]). Now, when God's enemy stands before Him, He cries to God, whose omnipotence He knows : 'All things are possible with thee ; let this cup pass from me' (Mark 14[36]). And when He concludes, 'Yet not as I will, but as thou wilt', this does not mean that at the last He, like Socrates, regards death as the friend, the liberator. No, He means only this : If this greatest of all terrors, death, must befall Me according to Thy will, then I submit to this horror. Jesus knows that in itself, because death is the enemy of God, to die means to be utterly forsaken. Therefore He cries to God; in face of this enemy of God He does not want to be alone. He wants to remain as closely tied to God as He has been throughout His whole earthly life. For whoever is in the hands of death is no longer in the hands of God, but in the hands of God's enemy. At this moment, Jesus seeks the assistance, not only of God, but even of His disciples. Again and again He interrupts His prayer and goes to His most intimate disciples, who are trying to fight off sleep in order to be awake when the men come to arrest their Master. They try; but they do not succeed, and Jesus must wake them again and again. Why does He want them to keep awake? He does not want to be alone. When the terrible enemy, death, approaches, He does not want to be forsaken even by the disciples whose human weakness He knows. 'Could you not watch one hour?' (Mark 14[37]).

Can there be a greater contrast than that between Socrates and Jesus? Like Jesus, Socrates has his disciples about him on the day of his death; but he discourses serenely with them on immortality. Jesus, a few hours before His death, trembles and begs His disciples not to leave Him alone. The author of the Epistle to the Hebrews, who, more than any other New Testament author, emphasizes the full deity (1[10]) but also the full humanity of Jesus, goes still farther than the reports of the three Synoptists in his description of Jesus' fear of death. In 5[7] he writes that Jesus 'with loud cries and tears offered up prayers and supplications to Him who was able to save Him'.[4] Thus, according to the Epistle to the Hebrews, Jesus wept and cried in the face of death. There is Socrates, calmly and composedly speaking of the immortality of the soul; here Jesus, weeping and crying.

And then the death-scene itself. With sublime calm Socrates drinks the hemlock; but Jesus (thus says the Evangelist, Mark 15[34]—we dare not gloss it over) cries: 'My God, my God, why hast thou forsaken me?' And with another inarticulate cry He dies (Mark 15[37]). This is not 'death as a friend'. This is death in all its frightful horror. This is really '*the last enemy*' of God. This is the name Paul gives it in 1 Corinthians 15[26], where the whole contrast between Greek thought and Christianity is disclosed.[5] Using different words, the author of the Johannine Apocalypse also regards death as the last enemy, when he describes how at the end death will be cast into the lake of fire (20[14]). Because it is God's enemy, it separates us from God, who is Life and the Creator of all life. Jesus, who is so closely tied to God, tied as no other man has even been, for precisely this reason must experience death much

[4] The reference to Gethsemane here seems to me unmistakable. J. Héring, *L'Epître aux Hébreux* (1954), ad loc., concurs in this.

[5] The problem is presented in entirely false perspective by J. Leipoldt, *Der Tod bei Griechen und Juden* (1942). To be sure, he correctly makes a sharp distinction between the Greek view of death and the Jewish. But Leipoldt's efforts always to equate the Christian with the Greek and oppose it to the Jewish only become comprehensible when one notes the year in which this book was published and the series (*Germanentum, Christentum und Judentum*) of which it is a part.

more terribly than any other man. To be in the hands of the great enemy of God means to be forsaken by God. In a way quite different from others, Jesus must suffer this abandonment, this separation from God, the only condition really to be feared. Therefore He cries to God: 'Why hast thou forsaken me?' He is now actually in the hands of God's great enemy.

We must be grateful to the Evangelists for having glossed over nothing at this point. Later (as early as the beginning of the second century, and probably even earlier) there were people who took offence at this—people of Greek provenance. In early Christian history we call them Gnostics.

I have put the death of Socrates and the death of Jesus side by side. For nothing shows better the radical difference between the Greek doctrine of the immortality of the soul and the Christian doctrine of the Resurrection. Because Jesus underwent death in all its horror, not only in His body, but also in His soul ('My God, why hast thou forsaken me'), and as He is regarded by the first Christians as the Mediator of salvation, He must indeed be the very one who in His death conquers death itself. He cannot obtain this victory by simply living on as an immortal soul, thus fundamentally *not* dying. He can conquer death only by actually dying, by betaking Himself to the sphere of death, the destroyer of life, to the sphere of 'nothingness', of abandonment by God. When one wishes to overcome someone else, one must enter his territory. Whoever wants to conquer death must die;

he must really cease to live—not simply live on as an immortal soul, but die in body and soul, lose life itself, the most precious good which God has given us. For this reason the Evangelists, who none the less intended to present Jesus as the Son of God, have not tried to soften the terribleness of His thoroughly human death.

Furthermore, if life is to issue out of so genuine a death as this, a new divine act of creation is necessary. And this act of creation calls back to life not just a part of the man, but the whole man—all that God had created and death had annihilated. For Socrates and Plato no new act of creation is necessary. For the body is indeed bad and should not live on. And that part which is to live on, the soul, does not die at all.

If we want to understand the Christian faith in the Resurrection, we must completely disregard the Greek thought that the material, the bodily, the corporeal is bad and *must* be destroyed, so that the death of the body would not be in any sense a destruction of the true life. For Christian (and Jewish) thinking the death of the body is *also* destruction of God-created life. No distinction is made: even the life of our body is true life; death is the destruction of *all* life created by God. Therefore it is death and not the body which must be conquered by the Resurrection.

Only he who apprehends with the first Christians the horror of death, who takes death seriously as death, can comprehend the Easter exultation of the primitive Christian community and understand that the whole thinking of the New Testament is governed by belief in the Resurrection. Belief in the immortality of the soul is not belief in a revolutionary event. Immortality, in fact, is only a *negative* assertion: the soul does *not* die, but simply lives on. Resurrection is a *positive* assertion: the whole man, who has really died, is recalled to life by a new act of creation by God. Something has happened—a miracle of creation! For something has also happened previously, something fearful: life formed by God has been destroyed.

Death in itself is not beautiful, not even the death of Jesus. Death before Easter is really the Death's head surrounded by the odour of decay. And the death of Jesus is as loathsome as the great painter Grünewald depicted it in the Middle Ages. But precisely for this reason the same painter understood how to paint, along with it, in an incomparable way, the great victory, the Resurrection of Christ: Christ in the new body, the Resurrection body. Whoever paints a pretty death can paint no resurrection. Whoever has not grasped the horror of death cannot join Paul in the hymn of victory: 'Death is swallowed up—in victory! O death, where is thy victory? O death, where is thy sting?' (1 Corinthians 15^{54f}).

II

THE WAGES OF SIN: DEATH

BODY AND SOUL—FLESH AND SPIRIT

YET THE contrast between the Greek idea of the immortality of the soul and the Christian belief in the resurrection is still deeper. The belief in the resurrection presupposes the Jewish connexion between death and *sin*. Death is not something natural, willed by God, as in the thought of the Greek philosophers; it is rather something unnatural, abnormal, opposed to God.[1] The Genesis narrative teaches us that it came into the world only by the sin of man. Death is a curse, and the whole creation has become involved in the curse. The sin of man has necessitated the whole series of events which the Bible records and which we call the story of redemption. Death can be conquered only to the extent that sin is removed. For 'death is the wages of sin'. It is not only the Genesis narrative which speaks thus. Paul says the same thing (Romans 6[23]), and this is the view of death held by the whole of primitive Christianity. Just as sin is something opposed to

[1] We shall see that Death, in view of its conquest by Christ, has lost all its horror. But I still would not venture as does Karl Barth, *Die Kirchliche Dogmatik*, III, 2 (1948), p. 777ff (on the basis of the 'second death' distinguished in Apocalypse 21[8]), to speak in the name of the New Testament of a 'natural death' (see 1 Corinthians 11[30]!).

God, so is its consequence, death. To be sure, God can make use of death (1 Corinthians 15[35ff], John 12[24]), as He can make use of Satan to man.

Nevertheless, death *as such* is the enemy of God. For God is Life and the Creator of life. It is not by the will of God that there are withering and decay, dying and sickness, the by-products of death working in our life. All these things, according to Christian and Jewish thinking, come from human sin. Therefore, every healing which Jesus accomplishes is not only a driving back of death, but also an invasion of the province of sin; and therefore on every occasion Jesus says: 'Your sins are forgiven.' Not as though there were a corresponding sin for every individual sickness; but rather, like the presence of death, the fact that sickness exists at all is a consequence of the sinful condition of the whole of humanity. Every healing is a partial resurrection, a partial victory of life over death. That is the Christian point of view. According to the Greek interpretation, on the contrary, bodily sickness is a corollary of the fact that the body is bad in itself and is ordained to destruction. For the Christian an anticipation of the Resurrection can already become visible, even in the earthly body.

That reminds us that the body is in no sense bad in itself, but is, like the soul, a gift of our Creator. Therefore, according to Paul, we have duties with regard to our body. God is the *Creator* of all things. The Greek doctrine of immortality and the Christian hope in the resurrection differ so radically because Greek thought has such an entirely different interpretation of creation. The Jewish and Christian interpretation of creation excludes the whole Greek dualism of body and soul. For indeed the visible, the corporeal, is just as truly God's creation as the visible. God is the maker of the body. The body is not the soul's prison, but rather a temple, as Paul says (1 Corinthians 6[19]) : the temple of the Holy Spirit! The basic distinction lies here. Body and soul are not opposites. God finds the corporeal 'good' after He has created it. The Genesis story makes this emphasis explicit. Conversely, moreover, sin also embraces the whole man, not only the body, but the soul as well; and its consequence, death, extends over all the rest of creation. Death is accordingly something dreadful, because the whole visible creation, including our body, is something wonderful, even if it is corrupted by sin and death. Behind the pessimistic interpretation of death stands the optimistic view of creation. Wherever, as in Platonism, death is thought of in terms of liberation, there the visible world is not recognized directly as God's creation.

Now, it must be granted that in Greek thought there is also a very positive appreciation of the body. But in Plato the good and beautiful in the corporeal are not good and beautiful in virtue of corporeality but rather, so to speak, *in spite of* corporeality : the soul, the eternal and the only substantial reality of being, shines faintly through the material. The corporeal is not the real, the eternal, the divine. It is merely that through which the real appears—and then only in debased form. The corporeal is meant to lead us to contemplate the pure archetype, freed from all corporeality, the invisible Idea.

To be sure, the Jewish and Christian points of view also see something else besides corporeality. For the whole creation is corrupted by sin and death. The creation which we see is not as God willed it, as He created it; nor is the body which we wear. Death rules over all; and it is not necessary for annihilation to accomplish its work of destruction before this fact becomes apparent—it is already obvious in the whole outward form of all things. Everything, even the most beautiful, is marked by death. Thus it might seem as if the distinction between Greek and Christian interpretation is not so great after all. And yet it remains radical. Behind the corporeal appearance Plato senses the incorporeal, transcendent, pure Idea. Behind the corrupted creation, under sentence of death, the Christian sees the future creation brought into being by the resurrection, just as God willed it. The contrast, for the Christian, is not between the body and the soul, not between outward form and Idea, but rather between the creation delivered over to death by sin and new creation; between the corruptible, fleshly body and the incorruptible resurrection body.

This leads us to a further point: the Christian interpretation of man. The anthropology of the New Testament is not Greek, but is connected with Jewish conceptions. For the concepts of body, soul, flesh, and spirit (to name only these), the New Testament does indeed use the same words as the Greek philosopher.

But they mean something quite different, and we understand the whole New Testament amiss when we construe these concepts only from the point of view of Greek thought. Many misunderstandings arise thus. I cannot present here a biblical anthropology in detail. There are good monographs on the subject,[2] not to mention the appropriate articles in the *Theologisches Wörterbuch*. A complete study would have to treat separately the anthropologies of the various New Testament authors, since on this point there exist differences which are by no means unimportant.[3] Of necessity I can deal here only with a few cardinal points which concern our problem, and even this must be done somewhat schematically, without taking into account the nuances which would have to be discussed in a proper anthropology. In so doing, we shall naturally have to rely primarily upon Paul, since only in his writings do we find an anthropology which is definable in detail, even though he too fails to use the different ideas with complete consistency.[4]

The New Testament certainly knows the difference between body and soul, or more precisely, between the inner and the outer man. This distinction does not,

[2] W. G. Kümmel, *Das Bild des Menschen im Neuen Testament* (1948).

[3] Also the various Theologies of the New Testament should here be mentioned.

[4] W. Gutbrod, *Die paulinische Anthropologie* (1934); W. G. Kümmel, *Römer 7 und die Bekehrung des Paulus* (1929); E. Schweitzer, 'Rom. 1[3f] und der Gegensatz von Fleisch und Geist vor und bei Paulus': *Evang. Theol.*, *15* (1955), pp. 563ff; and especially the relevant chapter in R. Bultmann, *Theology of the New Testament* (1955).

however, imply opposition, as if the one were by nature good, the other by nature bad.[5] Both belong together, both are created by God. The inner man without the outer has no proper, full existence. It requires a body. It can, to be sure, somehow lead a shady existence without the body, like the dead in Sheol according to the Old Testament, but that is not a *genuine life*. The contrast with the Greek soul is clear: it is precisely apart from the body that the Greek soul attains to full development of its life. According to the Christian view, however, it is the inner man's very nature which demands the body.

And what now is the role played by the flesh (σάρξ) and spirit (πνεῦμα)? Here it is especially important not to be misled by the secular use of the Greek words, though it is found in various places even in the New Testament and even within individual writers whose use of terminology is never completely uniform. With these reservations, we may say that according to the use which is characteristic, say, for Pauline theology, flesh and spirit in the New Testament are two *transcendent* powers which can enter into man from without; but *neither is given with human existence as such*. On the whole it is true that the Pauline anthropology, contrary to the Greek, is grounded in *Heilsgeschichte*.[6]

[5] Also the words of Jesus in Mark 8^{36}, Matthew 6^{25} and Matthew 10^{28} (ψυχή = life) do not speak of an 'infinite value of the immortal soul' and presuppose no higher valuation of the inner man. See also (also *re* Mark 14^{38}) Kümmel, *Das Bild des Menschen*, pp. 16ff.

[6] This is what Kümmel, *Das Bild des Menschen*, means when he states that in the New Testament, including the Johannine theology, man is always conceived as an *historical* being.

'Flesh' is the power of sin or the power of death. It seizes the outer and the inner man *together*. *Spirit* (πνεῦμα) is its great antagonist: the power of creation. It also seizes the outer and inner man *together*. Flesh and spirit are active powers, and as such they work within us. The flesh, the power of death, entered man with the sin of Adam; indeed it entered the whole man, inner and outer; yet in such a way that it is very closely linked with the body. The inner man finds itself less closely connected with the flesh;[7] although through guilt this power of death has more and more taken possession even of the inner man. The spirit, on the other hand, is the great power of life, the element of the resurrection; God's power of creation is given to us through the Holy Spirit. In the Old Testament the Spirit is at work only from time to time in the prophets. In the End-time in which we live—that is, since Christ has broken the power of death in His own death and has arisen—this power of life is at work in all members of the community (Acts 2^{16}: 'in the last days'). Like the flesh, it too already takes possession of the whole man, inner and outer. But whereas, in this age, the flesh has established itself to a substantial degree in the body, though it does not rule the inner man in the same inescapable way, the quickening

[7] The body is, so to speak, its locus, from which point it affects the whole man. This explains why Paul is able to speak of 'body' instead of 'flesh', or conversely 'flesh' instead of 'body', contrary to his own basic conception, although this occurs in very few passages. These terminological exceptions do not alter his general view, which is characterized by a sharp distinction between body and flesh.

power of the Holy Spirit is already taking possession of the inner man so decisively that the inner man is 'renewed from day to day', as Paul says (2 Corinthians 4^{16}). The whole Johannine Gospel emphasizes the point. We are already in the state of resurrection, that of eternal life—not immortality of soul: the new era is already inaugurated. The body, too, is already in the power of the Holy Spirit.

Wherever the Holy Spirit is at work we have what amounts to a momentary retreat of the power of death, a certain foretaste of the End.[8] This is true even in the body, hence the healings of the sick. But here it is a question only of a retreat, not of a final transformation of the body of death into a resurrection body. Even those whom Jesus raised up in His lifetime will die again, for they did not receive a resurrection body, the transformation of the fleshly body into a spiritual body does not take place until the End. Only then will the Holy Spirit's power of resurrection take such complete possession of the body that it transforms it in the way it is already transforming the inner man. It is important to see how different the New Testament anthropology is from that of the Greeks. Body and soul are both originally good in so far as they are created by God; they are both bad in so far as the deadly power of the flesh has hold of them. Both can and must be set free by the quickening power of the Holy Spirit.

[8] See my article, 'La délivrance anticipée du corps humain d'après le Nouveau Testament', *Hommage et Reconnaissance. 60e anniversaire de K. Barth* (1946), pp. 31ff.

Here, therefore, deliverance consists not in a release of soul from body but in a release of both from flesh. We are not released from the body; rather the body itself is set free. This is made especially clear in the Pauline Epistles, but it is the interpretation of the whole New Testament. In this connexion one does not find the differences which are present among the various books on other points. Even the much-quoted saying of Jesus in Matthew 10[28] in no way presupposes the Greek conception. 'Fear not them that kill the body, but cannot kill the soul.' It might seem to presuppose the view that the soul has no need of the body, but the context of the passage shows that this is not the case. Jesus does not continue: 'Be afraid of him who kills the soul'; rather: 'Fear him who can slay both soul *and* body in Gehenna.' That is, fear God, who is able to give you over completely to death; to wit, when He does not resurrect you to life. We shall see, it is true, that the soul is the starting-point of the resurrection, since, as we have said, it can already be possessed by the Holy Spirit in a way quite different from the body. The Holy Spirit already lives in our inner man. 'By the Holy Spirit who dwells in you (already)', says Paul in Romans 8[11], 'God will also quicken your mortal bodies.' Therefore, those who kill only the body are not to be feared. It can be raised from the dead. Moreover, it must be raised. The soul cannot always remain without a body. And on the other side we hear in Jesus' saying in Matthew 10[28] that the soul can be killed. The soul is not immortal. There must be resurrection for both; for since the Fall the whole man is 'sown corruptible'. For the inner man, thanks to the transformation by the quickening power of the Holy Spirit, the resurrection can take place already in this present life: through the 'renewal from day to day'. The flesh, however, still maintains its seat in our body. The transformation of the body does not take place until the End, when the whole creation will be made new by the Holy Spirit, when there will be no death and no corruption.

The resurrection of the body, whose substance[9] will no longer be that of the flesh, but that of the Holy Spirit, is only a part of the *whole new creation*. 'We wait for a new heaven *and* a new earth', says 2 Peter 3[13]. The Christian hope relates not only to my individual fate, but to the entire creation. Through sin the whole creation has become involved in death. This we hear not only in Genesis, but also in Romans 8[19ff], where Paul writes that the whole creation[10] from now on waits longingly for deliverance. This deliverance will come when the power of the Holy Spirit transforms all matter, when God in a new act of creation will not *destroy* matter, but set it free from the flesh, from corruptibility. Not eternal Ideas, but concrete objects will then rise anew, in the new, incorruptible life-substance

[9] I use this rather unfortunate term for want of a better. What I mean by it will be clear from the preceding discussion.

[10] The allusion in verse 20 to the words 'for your sake' of Genesis 3[17], excludes the translation of κτίσις as 'creature' in the sense of man, a translation advocated by E. Brunner and A. Schlatter. See O. Cullman, *Christ and Time* (1950), p. 103.

of the Holy Spirit; and among these objects belongs our body as well.

Because resurrection of the body is a new act of creation which embraces everything, it is not an event which begins with each individual death, but only at the *End*. It is not a transition from this world to another world, as is the case of the immortal soul freed from the body; rather it is the transition from the present age to the future. It is tied to the whole process of redemption.

Because there is sin there must be a process of redemption enacted in time. Where sin is regarded as the source of death's lordship over God's creation, there this sin and death must be vanquished together, and there the Holy Spirit, the only power able to conquer death, must win all creatures back to life in a continuous process.

Therefore the Christian belief in the resurrection, as distinct from the Greek belief in immortality, is tied to a *divine total process* implying deliverance. Sin and death must be conquered. *We* cannot do this. *Another* has done it for us; and He was able to do it only in that He betook himself to the province of death—that is, He himself died and expiated sin, so that death as the wages of sin is overcome. Christian faith proclaims that Jesus has done this and that He arose *with* body and soul after He was fully and really dead. Here God has consummated the miracle of the new creation expected at the End. Once again He has created life as in the beginning. At this one point, in Jesus Christ, this has already happened! Resurrection, not only in the sense of the Holy Spirit's taking possession of the *inner* man, but also resurrection of the *body*. This is a new creation of matter, an incorruptible matter. Nowhere else in the world is there this new spiritual matter. Nowhere else is there a spiritual body—only here in Christ.

III

THE FIRST-BORN FROM THE DEAD

BETWEEN THE RESURRECTION OF CHRIST AND THE DESTRUCTION OF DEATH

WE MUST take into account what it meant for the Christians when they proclaimed : Christ is risen from the dead ! Above all we must bear in mind what death meant for them. We are tempted to associate these powerful affirmations with the Greek thought of the immortality of the soul, and in this way to rob them of their content. Christ is risen : that is, we stand in the new era in which death is conquered, in which corruptibility is no more. For if there is really *one* spiritual body (not an immortal soul, but a spiritual body) which has emerged from a fleshly body, then indeed the power of death is broken. Believers, according to the conviction of the first Christians, should no longer die : this was certainly their expectation in the earliest days. It must have been a problem when they discovered that Christians continued to die. But even the fact that men continue to die no longer has the same significance after the Resurrection of Christ. The fact of death is robbed of its former significance. Dying is no longer an expression of the absolute lordship of Death, but only one of

Death's last contentions for lordship. Death cannot put an end to the great fact that there is *one* risen Body.

We ought to try simply to understand what the first Christians meant when they spoke of Christ as being the 'first-born from the dead'. However difficult it may be for us to do so, we must exclude the question whether or not we can accept this belief. We must also at the very start leave on one side the question whether Socrates or the New Testament is right. Otherwise we shall find ourselves continually mixing alien thought-processes with those of the New Testament. We should for once simply listen to what the New Testament says. Christ the first-born from the dead! His body the first Resurrection Body, the first Spiritual Body. Where this conviction is present, the whole of life and the whole of thought must be influenced by it. The whole thought of the New Testament remains for us a book sealed with seven seals if we do not read behind every sentence there this other sentence: Death has already been overcome (death, be it noted, not the body); there is already a new creation (a new creation, be it noted, not an immortality which the soul has always possessed) the resurrection age is already inaugurated.[1]

Granted that it is only inaugurated, but still it is *decisively* inaugurated. *Only* inaugurated: for death is

[1] If, as the Qumrân fragment most recently published by Allegro seems to confirm, the 'teacher of righteousness' of this sect really was put to death and his return was awaited, still what most decisively separates this sect from the original Christian community (apart from the other differences, for which see my article, 'The Significance of the Qumrân Texts', *J. B. L.*, 1955, pp. 213ff) is the absence in it of faith in a resurrection which has *already* occurred.

at work, and Christians still die. The disciples experienced this as the first members of the Christian community died. This necessarily presented them with a difficult problem.[2] In 1 Corinthians 11^{30} Paul writes that basically death and sickness should no longer occur. We still die, and still there is sickness and sin. But the Holy Spirit is already effective in our world as the power of new creation; He is already at work visibly in the primitive community in the diverse manifestations of the Spirit. In my book *Christ and Time* I have spoken of a tension between present and future, the tension between 'already fulfilled' and 'not yet consummated'. This tension belongs *essentially* to the New Testament and is not introduced as a secondary solution born of embarrassment,[3] as Albert Schweitzer's disciples and Rudolph Bultmann maintain.[4] This tension is already present in and with Jesus. He proclaims the Kingdom of God for the future; but on the other hand, He proclaims that the Kingdom of God has already broken in, since He Himself with the Holy Spirit is indeed already repulsing death by healing the sick and raising the dead (Matthew 12^{28}, 11^{3ff}, Luke

[2] See in this regard Ph. H. Menoud, 'La mort d'Ananias et de Saphira', *Aux sources de la tradition chrétienne. Melanges offerts à M. Goguel* (1950), particularly pp. 150ff.

[3] See particularly F. Buri, 'Das Problem des ausgebliebenen Parusie', *Schweiz. Theol. Umschau* (1946), pp. 97ff. See in addition O. Cullmann, 'Das wahre durch die ausgebliebene Parusie gestellte neutestamentliche Problem', *Theol. Zeitschr.* 3 (1947), p. 177ff; also pp. 428ff.

[4] R. Bultmann, 'History and Eschatology in the New Testament', *New Test. Stud.*, 1 (1954), pp. 5ff.

10[18]) in anticipation of the victory over death which He obtains in His own death. Schweitzer is not right when he sees as the original Christian hope *only* a hope in the future; nor is C. H. Dodd when he speaks *only* of realized eschatology; still less Bultmann when he resolves the original hope of Jesus and the first Christians into Existentialism. It belongs to the very stuff of the New Testament that it thinks in temporal categories, and this is because the belief that in Christ the resurrection is achieved is the starting-point of all Christian living and thinking. When one starts from this principle, then the chronological tension between 'already fulfilled' and 'not yet consummated' constitutes the *essence* of the Christian faith. Then the metaphor I use in *Christ and Time* characterizes the whole New Testament situation: the decisive battle has been fought in Christ's death and Resurrection; only V-day is yet to come.

Basically the whole contemporary theological discussion turns upon this question: Is *Easter* the starting-point of the Christian Church, of its existence, life, and thought? If so, we are living in an interim time.

In that case, the faith in resurrection of the New Testament becomes the cardinal point of all Christian belief. Accordingly, the fact that there is a resurrection body—Christ's body—defines the first Christians' whole interpretation of time. If Christ is the 'first-born from the dead', then this means that the End-time is already present. But it also means that a temporal interval separates the First-born from all other men who are not yet 'born from the dead'. This means then that we live in an interim time, between Jesus' Resurrection, which has already taken place, and our own, which will not take place until the End. It also means, moreover, that the quickening Power, the Holy Spirit, is already at work among us. Therefore Paul designates the Holy Spirit by the same term—*ἀπαρχή*, first-fruits (Romans 8[23])—as he uses for Jesus Himself (1 Corinthians 15[23]). There is then already a foretaste of the resurrection. And indeed in a twofold way: our inner man is already being renewed from day to day by the Holy Spirit (2 Corinthians 4[16]; Ephesians 3[16]); the body also has already been laid hold of by the Spirit, although the flesh still has its citadel within it. Wherever the Holy Spirit appears, the vanquished power of death recoils, even in the body. Hence miracles of healing occur even in our still mortal body. To the despairing cry in Romans 7[24], 'Who shall deliver me from this body of death?' the whole New Testament answers: The Holy Spirit!

The foretaste of the End, realized through the Holy Spirit, becomes most clearly visible in the early Christian celebration of the breaking of bread. Visible miracles of the Spirit occur there. There the Spirit tries to break through the limits of imperfect human language in the speaking with tongues. And there the community passes over into direct connexion with the Risen One, not only with His soul, but also with His Resurrection Body. Therefore we hear in 1 Corinthians 10[16]: 'The bread we break, is it not communion with the body of Christ?' Here in communion with the brethren we come nearest to the Resurrection Body of Christ; and so Paul writes in the following Chapter 11 (a passage which has received far too little consideration): if this Lord's Supper were partaken of by all members of the community in a completely worthy manner, then the union with Jesus' Resurrection Body would be so effective in our own bodies that even now there would be no more sickness or death (1 Corinthians 11^{28-30})—a singularly bold assertion.[5] Therefore the community is described as the body of Christ, because here the spiritual body of Christ is present, because here we come closest to it; here in the common meal the first disciples at Easter saw Jesus' Resurrection Body, His Spiritual Body.

Yet in spite of the fact that the Holy Spirit is already so powerfully at work, men still die; even after Easter and Pentecost men continue to die as before. Our body remains mortal and subject to sickness. Its transformation into the spiritual body does not take place until the whole creation is formed anew by God. Then only, for the first time, there will be nothing but Spirit, nothing but the power of life, for then death will be destroyed with finality. Then there will be a new substance for all things visible. Instead of the fleshly matter there appears the spiritual. That is, *instead of corruptible matter there appears the incorruptible*. The

[5] F. J. Leenhardt's new study, *Ceci est mon corps. Explication de ces paroles de Jésus-Christ* (1955), is also to be understood in the light of this.

visible and the invisible will be spirit. But let us make no mistake: this is certainly not the Greek sense of bodiless Idea! A new heaven *and* a new earth! That is the Christian hope. And then will our bodies also rise from the dead. Yet not as fleshly bodies, but as spiritual bodies.

The expression which stands in the ancient Greek texts of the Apostles' Creed is quite certainly not biblical: 'I believe in the resurrection of the flesh!'[6] Paul could not say that. Flesh and blood cannot inherit the Kingdom. Paul believes in the resurrection of the *body*, not of the *flesh*. The flesh is the power of death, which must be destroyed. This error in the Greek creed made its entrance at a time when the biblical terminology had been misconstrued in the sense of Greek anthropology. Our body, moreover (not merely our soul), will be raised at the End, when the quickening power of the Spirit makes all things new, all things without exception.

An incorruptible body! How are we to conceive this? Or better, how did the first Christians conceive of it? Paul says in Philippians 3[21] that at the End Christ will transform our lowly body into the body of his own glory (δόξα), just as in 2 Corinthians 3[18]: 'We are being transformed into his own likeness from glory to glory (ἀπὸ δόξης εἰς δόξαν)' This glory (δόξα) was conceived by the first Christians as a sort of

[6] W. Bieder, 'Auferstehung des Leibes oder des Fleisches?', *Theol. Zeitschrift*, 1 (1945), pp. 105ff, seeks to explicate the expression 'resurrection of the flesh' both from the point of view of biblical theology and of the history of dogma.

light-substance; but this is only an imperfect comparison. Our language has no word for it. Once again I refer to Grünewald's painting of the Resurrection. He may have come closest to what Paul understood as the spiritual body.

IV

THOSE WHO SLEEP

THE HOLY SPIRIT AND THE INTERMEDIATE STATE OF THE DEAD

AND NOW WE come to the last question. When does this transformation of the body take place? No doubt can remain on this point. The whole New Testament answers, at the *End*, and this is to be understood literally, that is, in the temporal sense. That raises the question of the 'interim condition' of the dead. Death is indeed already conquered according to 2 Timothy 1^{10}: 'Christ has conquered death and has already brought life and incorruptibility to light.' The chronological tension which I constantly stress, concerns precisely this central point: death is conquered, but it will not be abolished until the End. According to 1 Corinthians 15^{26}, death will be conquered as the *last enemy*. It is significant that in the Greek the same verb καταργέω[1] is used to describe both the decisive victory already accomplished and the not-yet-consummated victory at the end. John's Apocalypse 20^{14} describes the victory at the end, the annihilation of Death: 'Death will be cast into a pool of fire'; and a few verses farther on it is said, 'Death will be no more'.

[1] Luther translates καταργέω by 'er hat ihm "die Macht genommen"' in 2 Timothy 1^{10}, and by 'er wird aufgehoben' in 1 Corinthians 15^{26}.

[illegible] is [illegible] life, as he takes away sin, which destroys life, and brings death

IMPORTANT.

CHECKER........................PACKER.......................REF............

In the event of any complaint or of goods arriving in a damaged condition, or not being in accord with your order please return this slip with full particulars to:—

FRANK H. CUMBERS,
25-35 City Road,
London, E.C.I.

NATURE OF COMPLAINT ....

....

....

NAME...

ADDRESS...

....

DATE....................................

That means, however, that the transformation of the body does not occur immediately after each individual death. Here too we must once again guard against any accommodation to Greek philosophy, if we wish to understand the New Testament doctrine. This is the point where I cannot accept Karl Barth's position as a simple restatement of the original Christian view, not even his position in the *Church Dogmatics*[2] where it is subtly shaded and comes much nearer[3] to New Testament eschatology than in his first writings.[4] Karl Barth considers it to be the New Testament interpretation that the transformation of the body occurs for everyone immediately after his individual death—as if the dead were no longer in time. Nevertheless, according to the New Testament, they *are* still in time. Otherwise, the problem in 1 Thessalonians 4[13ff] would have no meaning. Here in fact Paul is concerned to show

[2] K. Barth, *Die Kirchliche Dogmatik*, II, 1 (1940), pp. 698ff; III, 2 (1948), pp. 524ff, 714ff.

[3] It is another question, of course, whether Barth does not have the *right* to adduce relationships in this whole matter which yet lie outside the New Testament circle of vision. But if so, then this 'going beyond the New Testament' should perhaps be done consciously and should always be identified as such with clarity and emphasis, especially where a constant effort is being made to argue from the point of view of the Bible, as is the case with Barth. If this were done, then the inevitable danger which every dogmatician *must* confront (and here lies the dignity and greatness of his task) would be more clearly recognized: namely, the danger that he may not remain upon an extension of the biblical line, but rather interpret the biblical texts primarily *ex post facto*, from the point of view of his 'going beyond the New Testament'. Precisely because of this clear recognition of the danger, discussion with the exegete would be more fruitful.

[4] Especially *The Resurrection of the Dead* (1926).

that at the moment of Christ's return 'those who are then alive will have no advantage' over those who have died in Christ. Therefore the dead in Christ are still in time; they, too, are *waiting*. 'How long, oh Lord?' cry the martyrs who are sleeping under the altar in John's Apocalypse (6[11]). Neither the saying on the Cross, 'Today you will be with me in paradise' (Luke 23[43]), the parable of the rich man, where Lazarus is carried directly to Abraham's bosom (Luke 16[22]), nor Paul's saying, 'I desire to die and to be with Christ' (Philippians 1[23]), proves as is often maintained that the resurrection of the body takes place immediately after the individual death.[5] In none of these texts is there so

[5] Also the much-disputed words of Luke 22[43], 'Today you will be with me in Paradise', belong here. To be sure it is not impossible, though artificial, to understand *σήμερον* as modifying *λέγω σοι*. The statement is to be understood in the light of Luke 16[23] and of the late-Jewish conception of 'Paradise' as the place of the blessed (Strack-Billerbeck, ad. loc.; P. Volz, *Die Eschatologie der jüdischen Gemeinde im neutest. Zeitalter* (2nd Edn, 1934), p. 265). It is certain that Luke 16[23] does not refer to resurrection of the body, and the expectation of the *Parousia* is in no way supplanted. Such an interpretation is also decisively rejected by W. G. Kümmel, *Verheissung und Erfüllung*, 2nd Edn (1953), p. 67. A certain disparity here over against Pauline theology does exist in so far as Christ Himself on the day referred to as 'today' has not yet risen, and therefore the foundation of the condition wherein the dead are bound up with Christ has not yet been laid. But in the last analysis the emphasis here is on the fact that the thief will be *with Christ*. Menoud (*Le sort des trépassés*, p. 45) correctly points out that Jesus' answer must be understood in relation to the thief's entreaty. The thief asks Jesus to remember him when He 'comes into His kingdom', which according to the Jewish view of the Messiah can only refer to the time when the Messiah *will come* and erect his kingdom. Jesus does not grant the request, but instead gives the thief more than he asked for: he will be united *with Jesus* even before the coming of the kingdom. So understood, *according to their intention*, these words do not constitute a difficulty for the position maintained above.

much as a word about the resurrection of the body. Instead, these different images picture the condition of those who die in Christ before the End—the interim state in which they, as well as the living, find themselves. All these images express simply a special proximity to Christ, in which those dying in Christ before the End find themselves. They are 'with Christ' or 'in paradise' or 'in Abraham's bosom' or, according to Revelation 6^9, 'under the altar'. All these are simply various images of special nearness to God. But the most usual image for Paul is : 'They are asleep.'[6] It would be difficult to dispute that the New Testament reckons with such an interim time for the dead, as well as for the living, although any sort of speculation upon the state of the dead in this interim period is lacking here.

The dead in Christ share in the tension of the interim time.[7] But this means not *only* that they are waiting. It means that for them, too, something decisive happened with Jesus' death and Resurrection. For them, too, Easter is the great turning point (Matthew 27^{52}). This new situation created by Easter leads us to

[6] The interpretation which K. Barth (*Die Kirchliche Dogmatik*, III, 2, p. 778) gives of the 'sleeping', as if this term conveyed only the 'impression' of a peaceful going to sleep which those surviving have, finds no support in the New Testament. The expression in the New Testament signifies more, and like the 'repose' in Apocalypse 14^{13} refers to the *condition* of the dead before the Parousia.

[7] The lack of New Testament speculation on this does not give us the right simply to suppress the 'interim condition' as such. I do not understand why Protestant theologians (including Barth) are so afraid of the New Testament position when the New Testament teaches only this much about the 'interim condition': (1) that it exists, (2) that it already signifies union with Christ (this because of the Holy Spirit).

see at least the possibility of a common bond with Socrates, not with his teaching, but with his own behaviour in the face of death. Death has lost its horror, its 'sting'. Though it remains as the last enemy, Death has no longer any final significance. If the Resurrection of Christ were to designate the great turning-point of the ages only for the living and not for the dead also, then the living would surely have an immense advantage over the dead. For as members of Christ's community the living are indeed even now in possession of the power of the resurrection, the Holy Spirit. It is unthinkable that, according to the early Christian point of view, nothing should be altered for the dead in the period before the End. It is precisely those images used in the New Testament to describe the condition of the dead in Christ which prove that even now, in this interim state of the dead, the Resurrection of Christ—the anticipation of the End—is already effective. They are 'with Christ'.

Particularly in 2 Corinthians 5^{1-10} we hear why it is that the dead, although they do not yet have a body and are only 'sleeping', nevertheless are in special proximity to Christ. Paul speaks here of the natural anxiety which even he feels before death, which still maintains its effectiveness. He fears the condition of 'nakedness', as he calls it; that is, the condition of the inner man who has no body. This natural dread of death, therefore, has not disappeared. Paul would like, as he says, to receive a spiritual body in addition, directly (ἐπενδύσασθαι) while still living, without undergoing death. That is, he would like to be still alive at the time of Christ's return. Here once again we find confirmation of what we said about Jesus' fear of death. But now we see also something *new*: in this same text alongside this natural anxiety about the soul's nakedness stands the great confidence in Christ's proximity, *even in this interim state*. What is there to be afraid of in the fact that such an interim condition still exists? Confidence in Christ's proximity is grounded in the conviction that our inner man is already grasped by the Holy Spirit. Since the time of Christ, we, the living, do indeed have the Holy Spirit. If He is actually within us, He has already transformed our inner man. But, as we have heard, the Holy Spirit is the power of life. Death can do Him no harm. Therefore something is indeed changed for the dead, for those who really die in Christ, i.e. in possession of the Holy Spirit. The horrible abandonment in death, the separation from God, of which we have spoken, no longer exists, precisely because the Holy Spirit does exist. Therefore the New Testament emphasizes that the dead are indeed *with Christ*, and so not abandoned. Thus we understand how it is that, just in 2 Corinthians 5^{1ff}, where he mentions the fear of disembodiment in the interim time, Paul describes the Holy Spirit as the 'earnest'.

According to verse 8 of the same chapter, it even appears that the dead are nearer Christ. The 'sleep' seems to draw them even closer: 'We are willing rather to be absent from the body, and to be at home with the Lord.' For this reason, the apostle can write in Phil. 1[23] that he longs to die and be with Christ. So then, a man who lacks the fleshly body is yet nearer Christ than before, if he has the Holy Spirit. It is the flesh, bound to our earthly body, which is throughout our life the hindrance to the Holy Spirit's full development. Death delivers us from this hindrance even though it is an imperfect state inasmuch as it lacks the resurrection body. Neither in this passage nor elsewhere is found any more detailed information about this intermediate state in which the inner man, stripped indeed of its fleshly body but still deprived of the spiritual body, exists with the Holy Spirit. The apostle limits himself to assuring us that this state, anticipating the destiny which is ours once we have received the Holy Spirit, brings us closer to the final resurrection.

Here we find fear of a bodiless condition associated with firm confidence that even in this intermediate, transient condition no separation from Christ supervenes (among the powers which cannot separate us from the love of God in Christ is death—Romans 8[38]). This fear *and* this confidence are bound together in 2 Corinthians 5, and this confirms the fact that even the dead share in the present tension. Confidence predominates, however, for the decision has indeed been made. Death is conquered. The inner man, divested of the body, in no longer alone; he does not lead the shadowy existence which the Jews expected and which cannot be described as life. The inner man, divested of the body, has already in his lifetime been transformed by the Holy Spirit, is already grasped by the resurrection (Romans 6^{3ff}, John 3^{3ff}), if he *has* already as a living person really been renewed by the Holy Spirit. Although he still 'sleeps' and still awaits the resurrection of the body, which alone will give him full life, the dead Christian *has* the Holy Spirit. Thus, even in this state, death has lost its terror, although it still exists. And so the dead who die in the Lord can actually be blessed 'from now on' (ἀπ' ἄρτι),[8] as the author of the Johannine Apocalypse says (14^{13}). What is said in 1 Corinthians $15^{54b, 55}$ pertains also to the dead: 'Death is swallowed up in victory. O death, where is thy victory? O death, where is thy sting?' So the Apostle in Romans 14 writes: 'Whether we live or die, we belong to the Lord' (verse 8). Christ is 'Lord of the living and the dead' (verse 9).

One could ask whether in this fashion we have not been led back again, in the last analysis, to the Greek doctrine of immortality, whether the New Testament does not assume, for the time after Easter, a continuity of the 'inner Man' of converted people before and after

[8] In view of the places in the New Testament where ἀπ' ἄρτι can only mean 'from now on' (for instance, John 13^{19}), and in view of the good sense which the sentence makes when ἀπ' ἄρτι is so translated, I continue to subscribe to the usual translation 'from now on' and see it as modifying ἀποθνήσκοντες, although many factors support A. Debrunner's view, *Grammatik des neutest. Griechisch* (1943), Part II, Appendix, § 12, following A. Fridrichsen's suggestion, which understands ἀπαρτί as the colloquial Attic word for 'exactly, certainly' and then finds in P⁴⁷'s omission of ναί a support for reading ἀπ' ἄρτι as ἀπαρτί, modifying λέγει τὸ πνεῦμα, not ἀποθνήσκοντες.

death, so that here, too, death is presented for all practical purposes only as a natural 'transition'.[9] There is a sense in which a kind of *approximation* to the Greek teaching does actually take place, to the extent that the inner man, who has already been transformed by the Spirit (Romans 6^{3ff}), and consequently made alive, continues to live with Christ in this transformed state, in the condition of sleep. This continuity is emphasized especially strongly in the Gospel of John (3^{36}, 4^{14}, 6^{54}, and frequently). Here we observe at least a certain analogy to the 'immortality of the soul', but the distinction remains none the less radical. Further, the condition of the dead in Christ is still imperfect, a state of 'nakedness', as Paul says, of 'sleep', of waiting for the resurrection of the whole creation, for the resurrection of the body. On the other hand, death in the New Testament continues to be the enemy, albeit a defeated enemy, who must yet be destroyed. The fact that even in this state the dead are already living with Christ does not correspond to the natural essence of the soul. Rather it is the result of a divine intervention from outside, through the Holy Spirit, who must already have quickened the inner man in earthly life by His miraculous power.

Thus it is still true that the resurrection of the body is awaited, even in John's Gospel—though now, of course, with a certainty of victory because the Holy

[9] We have already spoken above of K. Barth's attempt (which indeed goes too far) to place a positive valuation in dialectical fashion alongside the negative valuation of death.

Spirit already dwells in the inner man. Hence no doubt can arise any more: since He already dwells in the inner man, He will certainly transform the body. For the Holy Spirit, this quickening power, penetrates everything and knows no barrier. If He is really within a man, then He will quicken the whole man. So Paul writes in Romans 8¹¹: 'If the Spirit dwells in you, then will He who raised Christ Jesus from the dead call to life your mortal bodies also *through the Spirit dwelling in you*.' In Philippians 3²¹: 'We wait for the Lord Jesus Christ, who will conform our lowly body to the body of His glory.' Nothing is said in the New Testament about the details of the interim conditions. We hear only this: we are nearer to God.

We wait, and *the dead* wait. Of course the rhythm of time may be different for them than for the living; and in this way the interim-time may be shortened for them. This does not, indeed, go beyond the New Testament texts and their exegesis,[10] because this expression *to sleep*, which is the customary designation in the New Testament of the 'interim condition', draws us to the view that for the dead another time-consciousness exists, that of 'those who sleep'. But that does not mean that the dead are not still in time. Therefore once again we see that the New Testament resurrection hope is different from the Greek belief in immortality.

[10] Here I follow R. Mehl's suggestion, *Der letzte Feind*, p. 56.

CONCLUSION

On his missionary journeys Paul surely met people who were unable to believe in his preaching of the resurrection *for the very reason* that they believed in the immortality of the soul. Thus in Athens there was no laughter until Paul spoke of the resurrection (Acts 17[32]). Both the people of whom Paul says (in 1 Thessalonians 4[13]) that 'they have no hope' and those of whom he writes (in 1 Corinthians 15[12]) that they do not believe there is a resurrection from the dead are probably not Epicureans, as we are inclined to believe. Even those who believe in the immortality of the soul do not have *the* hope of which Paul speaks, the hope which expresses the belief of a divine miracle of new creation which will embrace everything, every part of the world created by God. Indeed for the Greeks who believed in the immortality of the soul it may have been harder to accept the Christian preaching of the resurrection than it was for others. About the year 150 Justin (in his *Dialogue*, 80) writes of people, 'who say that there is no resurrection from the dead, but that immediately at death their souls would ascend to heaven'. Here the contrast is indeed clearly perceived.

The Emperor Marcus Aurelius, the philosopher who belongs with Socrates to the noblest figures of antiquity, also perceived the contrast. As is well known, he had the deepest contempt for Christianity.

One might think that the death of the Christian martyrs would have inspired respect in this great Stoic who regarded death with equanimity. But it was just the martyrs' death with which he was least sympathetic. The alacrity with which the Christians met their death displeased him.[1] The Stoic departed this life dispassionately; the Christian martyr on the other hand died with spirited passion for the cause of Christ, because he knew that by doing so he stood within a powerful redemptive process. The first Christian martyr, Stephen, shows us (Acts 7[55]) how very differently death is bested by him who dies in Christ than by the ancient philosopher: he sees, it is said, 'the heavens open and Christ standing at the right hand of God!' He sees Christ, the Conqueror of Death. With this faith that the death he must undergo is already conquered by Him who has Himself endured it, Stephen lets himself be stoned.

The answer to the question, 'Immortality of the soul or resurrection of the dead in the New Testament', is unequivocal. The *teaching* of the great philosophers Socrates and Plato can in no way be brought into consonance with that of the New Testament. That their *person*, their *life*, and their *bearing in death* can none the less be *honoured* by Christians, the apologists of the second century have shown. I believe it can also be demonstrated from the New Testament. But this is a question with which we do not have to deal here.

[1] M. Aurelius, *Med.*, XI, 3. To be sure, as time went on he more and more gave up the belief in the soul's immortality.

Body a prison for Ghr... Temple for Paul. p. 30.